Presented to

_____

By

_____

On the Occasion of

_____

Date

_____

GOD'S GIFTS
FOR THE
GRAD

Joanna Bloss

BARBOUR
PUBLISHING

ISBN 978-1-60260-378-3

Published by Barbour Publishing, Inc., P.O. Box 719, Uhrichsville, Ohio 44683, www.barbourbooks.com

Our mission is to publish and distribute inspirational products offering exceptional value and biblical encouragement to the masses.

Member of the
Evangelical Christian
Publishers Association

Printed in the United States of America.

Contents

Congratulations!

You've just achieved a major goal—graduation! All of your hard work has finally paid off and you definitely deserve a pat on the back. Good job.

Hopefully you know more today than you did when you started. An education is a great gift. It opens doors that would otherwise never be open. It gives us power to change our circumstances and can increase our influence with others. It provides us with myriad opportunities to change the world.

But have you noticed that the more you learn, the more you realize how much more there is to learn? We could spend the rest of our lives going to school, and yet the knowledge we'd acquire would be just a drop in the vast ocean of all there is to know.

Karl Barth was one of the most influential theologians of the twentieth century. This highly educated man studied at some of the world's finest universities and wrote volumes of complex theological material. In 1962, Barth visited the United States and someone asked him if he could sum up the essence of all he had written.

His reply?

"Jesus loves me, this I know, for the Bible tells me so."

Simple words, but their message is incredibly profound. No matter where your education takes you, don't ever lose sight of the beauty and simplicity of God's Word—His gift to you for today and for the rest of your life.

Positively Angry

*People with understanding control their anger;
a hot temper shows great foolishness.*
PROVERBS 14:29 NLT

Tara's day had been terrible. First her car wouldn't start, then she missed an important deadline at work. Her lunch sandwich was soggy, and once again her roommate failed to take out the garbage. Welcome cockroaches. So when her brother, Joe, showed up twenty minutes late for their mom's birthday dinner, Tara unleashed the fury of her rotten day on him.

"How dare you come in like you don't have a care in the world?" she hissed. "I've had to sit here entertaining Mom while you're off doing who knows what—" The look on her brother's face stopped Tara short.

"I'm sorry," he said. "My friend Matt called as I was walking out the door." Joe paused. "His cancer is back."

Have you ever unleashed your anger on someone before you had all the information? Proverbs says that controlling our anger requires great understanding. Controlling our anger means seeing the situation through the other person's eyes—before we jump to conclusions. It means thinking before we speak. It means asking questions before we make assumptions. While anger can be an appropriate and helpful emotion, it is always better to keep it under control—and one of the first steps is getting all the information.

Don't sin by letting anger control you.
Think about it overnight and remain silent.
PSALM 4:4 NLT

An angry person starts fights;
a hot-tempered person commits all kinds of sin.
PROVERBS 29:22 NLT

Cease from anger, and forsake wrath;
do not fret—it only causes harm.
PSALM 37:8 NKJV

Wrath kills a foolish man,
and envy slays a simple one.
JOB 5:2 NKJV

Smart people know how to hold their tongue;
their grandeur is to forgive and forget.
PROVERBS 19:11 MSG

The wrath of God is being revealed from heaven
against all the godlessness and wickedness of men
who suppress the truth by their wickedness.
ROMANS 1:18 NIV

Slowness to anger makes for deep understanding;
a quick-tempered person stockpiles stupidity.
PROVERBS 14:29 MSG

Control your temper,
for anger labels you a fool.
ECCLESIASTES 7:9 NLT

"Be angry, and do not sin": do not let the sun go down
on your wrath, nor give place to the devil.
EPHESIANS 4:26–27 NKJV

A fool is quick-tempered,
but a wise person stays calm when insulted.
PROVERBS 12:16 NLT

What I want mostly is for men to pray—not shaking
angry fists at enemies but raising holy hands to God.
1 TIMOTHY 2:8 MSG

Do not take revenge, my friends,
but leave room for God's wrath, for it is written:
"It is mine to avenge; I will repay," says the Lord.
ROMANS 12:19 NIV

Whoever sows sin reaps weeds,
and bullying anger sputters into nothing.
PROVERBS 22:8 MSG

Get rid of all bitterness, rage and anger, brawling
and slander, along with every form of malice.
EPHESIANS 4:31 NIV

Everyone should be quick to listen, slow to speak and
slow to become angry, for man's anger does not bring
about the righteous life that God desires.
JAMES 1:19–20 NIV

A man of great wrath will suffer punishment;
for if you rescue him, you will have to do it again.
PROVERBS 19:19 NKJV

CONVERSATION

These Words Could Use a Little Salt

Let your conversation be always full of grace, seasoned with salt,
so that you may know how to answer everyone.
COLOSSIANS 4:6 NIV

One of your coworkers wants to take a long lunch with his girlfriend. If the boss notices, he wonders if you will cover for him—saying something like he called to say his car broke down and he's running late?

What do you say? How about: *"If you think I'm going to lie for you, think again. There's no way I'm going to jeopardize my job for you."* Or how about this? *"Hey, Rick, I don't feel comfortable saying something that isn't true. Can I help you figure out how to get your project done so you can leave for an early dinner instead?"*

One response puts your coworker on the defensive. The other response is equally straightforward, but it opens the door for future conversations and gives you an opportunity to help instead of criticize.

Colossians says our words should be "full of grace . . .[as if they are] seasoned with salt." Throughout Jesus' earthly ministry, He seasoned His words with just the right amount of grace. He never concealed the truth, but when He spoke, He put the needs of His listeners first.

Grace. Like salt on our food, it improves the flavor of our words and prevents us from saying things we might regret later. How can you season your words with grace today?

*Do not let any unwholesome talk come out
of your mouths, but only what is helpful for
building others up according to their needs,
that it may benefit those who listen.*
EPHESIANS 4:29 NIV

*Too much talk leads to sin.
Be sensible and keep your mouth shut.*
PROVERBS 10:19 NLT

*It only takes a spark, remember, to set off a forest fire.
A careless or wrongly placed word out
of your mouth can do that.*
JAMES 3:5–6 MSG

*"You must give an account on judgment day for every
idle word you speak. The words you say will
either acquit you or condemn you."*
MATTHEW 12:36–37 NLT

A man has joy by the answer of his mouth,
and a word spoken in due season, how good it is!
PROVERBS 15:23 NKJV

If you claim to be religious but don't control your tongue,
you are fooling yourself, and your religion is worthless.
JAMES 1:26 NLT

A soft answer turns away wrath,
but a harsh word stirs up anger.
PROVERBS 15:1 NKJV

"If you want to enjoy life and see many happy days,
keep your tongue from speaking evil
and your lips from telling lies."
1 PETER 3:10 NLT

You must rid yourselves of all such things as these: anger, rage, malice, slander, and filthy language from your lips.
COLOSSIANS 3:8 NIV

He who guards his mouth and his tongue keeps himself from calamity.
PROVERBS 21:23 NIV

Do not speak evil of one another, brethren. He who speaks evil of a brother and judges his brother, speaks evil of the law and judges the law. But if you judge the law, you are not a doer of the law but a judge.
JAMES 4:11 NKJV

As a north wind brings rain, so a sly tongue brings angry looks.
PROVERBS 25:23 NIV

The words of a wise person are gracious.
The talk of a fool self-destructs.
ECCLESIASTES 10:12 MSG

There is gold and a multitude of rubies,
but the lips of knowledge are a precious jewel.
PROVERBS 20:15 NKJV

Though some tongues just love the taste of gossip,
those who follow Jesus have better uses for language
than that. Don't talk dirty or silly. That kind of talk
doesn't fit our style. Thanksgiving is our dialect.
EPHESIANS 5:3–4 MSG

Do you see a man hasty in his words?
There is more hope for a fool than for him.
PROVERBS 29:20 NKJV

COURAGE

The Lord Is with You

*"Be strong and courageous, and do the work.
Don't be afraid or discouraged, for the LORD God,
my God, is with you. He will not fail you or forsake you."*
1 CHRONICLES 28:20 NLT

For Theresa, it had been a long summer. Her grandmother passed away after a lengthy battle with cancer, and her relationship with her parents was strained. She was getting ready to start graduate school, and money was tight. With her future looming before her like a giant mountain, Theresa wasn't at all sure she had the strength to climb it.

Perhaps you know how Theresa feels. Whether it's job or money troubles, relationship difficulties, or just a bad day, it is all too easy to get discouraged by the size of the tasks that lie ahead.

David spoke the words in 1 Chronicles 28:20 to the Israelites, who were no doubt overwhelmed by *their* task, which was to build God's temple. David spoke the truth—God was with them, and with His help the Israelites successfully climbed that mountain.

Perhaps you're standing at the base of a giant mountain, looking at the rocks above and the steep climb ahead and wondering how on earth you're ever going to make it. Have courage! God promises to go before you and enable you to do things that seem beyond your abilities and strength.

So what are you waiting for? It's time to get your hiking shoes.

But Jesus spoke to them at once.
"Don't be afraid," he said.
"Take courage. I am here!"
MATTHEW 14:27 NLT

Wait on the LORD; be of good courage, and He shall
strengthen your heart; wait, I say, on the LORD!
PSALM 27:14 NKJV

Be on guard. Stand firm in the faith.
Be courageous. Be strong.
1 CORINTHIANS 16:13 NLT

So we say with confidence, "The Lord is my helper;
I will not be afraid. What can man do to me?"
HEBREWS 13:6 NIV

For God has not given us a spirit of fear,
but of power and of love and of a sound mind.
2 TIMOTHY 1:7 NKJV

In the fear of the LORD there is strong confidence,
and His children will have a place of refuge.
PROVERBS 14:26 NKJV

Be on your guard; stand firm in the faith;
be men of courage; be strong.
1 CORINTHIANS 16:13 NIV

Be brave. Be strong. Don't give up.
Expect God to get here soon.
PSALM 31:24 MSG

I can do all things through Christ who strengthens me.
PHILIPPIANS 4:13 NKJV

For the LORD will be your confidence
and will keep your foot from being snared.
PROVERBS 3:26 NIV

So, friends, we can now—without hesitation—walk
right up to God, into "the Holy Place." Jesus has cleared
the way by the blood of his sacrifice, acting as our priest
before God. The "curtain" into God's presence is his body.
HEBREWS 10:19 MSG

The LORD God is my strength;
He will make my feet like deer's feet,
and He will make me walk on my high hills.
HABAKKUK 3:19 NKJV

"Be strong. Take courage. Don't be intimidated. Don't give them a second thought because GOD, your God, is striding ahead of you. He's right there with you. He won't let you down; he won't leave you."
DEUTERONOMY 31:6 MSG

"Fear nothing in the things you're about to suffer— but stay on guard! Fear nothing! . . . Don't quit, even if it costs you your life. Stay there believing. I have a Life-Crown sized and ready for you."
REVELATION 2:10 MSG

"Do not be afraid, little flock, for your Father has been pleased to give you the kingdom."
LUKE 12:32 NIV

And so, dear brothers and sisters, we can boldly enter heaven's Most Holy Place because of the blood of Jesus.
HEBREWS 10:19 NLT

Now What?

*Neither height nor depth, nor anything else in all creation,
will be able to separate us from the love of God
that is in Christ Jesus our Lord.*
ROMANS 8:39 NIV

John hung up the phone, grateful his roommate was out for the evening. His dad just dropped a bombshell—how could his parents be divorcing after all these years? If they couldn't make it, how could anyone? Throughout the night, John wrestled with his feelings and cried out to God. He felt as if the very foundation of his world had been shattered. *What am I supposed to do now?* he wondered.

Has the foundation of your world ever been shattered? Perhaps, like John, you've received news that your parents are splitting up. That you didn't pass an important exam. That someone you thought was a friend turned out to be an enemy. Life can deal some pretty harsh blows sometimes.

Situations like these can cause us to question God's love. Why would a loving God let us suffer in this way? Unfortunately, there are no easy answers. However, we can rest on one solid truth—God is in control. He loves you. Nothing can change that. Your world could be caving in right now, but there is nothing that can ever separate you from God's love. Rest in Him.

The LORD is good, a stronghold in the day of trouble;
and He knows those who trust in Him.
NAHUM 1:7 NKJV

These hard times are small potatoes compared to the
coming good times, the lavish celebration prepared for
us. There's far more here than meets the eye. The things
we see now are here today, gone tomorrow. But the
things we can't see now will last forever.
2 CORINTHIANS 4:17–18 MSG

What then shall we say to these things?
If God is for us, who can be against us?
ROMANS 8:31 NKJV

That is why we never give up. Though our bodies are
dying, our spirits are being renewed every day.
2 CORINTHIANS 4:16 NLT

"Have I not commanded you? Be strong and of good courage; do not be afraid, nor be dismayed, for the LORD your God is with you wherever you go."
JOSHUA 1:9 NKJV

Because of the LORD's great love we are not consumed, for his compassions never fail. They are new every morning; great is your faithfulness.
LAMENTATIONS 3:22–23 NIV

He gives power to the weak and strength to the powerless.
ISAIAH 40:29 NLT

No one whose hope is in you will ever be put to shame.
PSALM 25:3 NIV

When you go through deep waters, I will be with you.
When you go through rivers of difficulty, you will not
drown. When you walk through the fire of oppression, you
will not be burned up; the flames will not consume you.
ISAIAH 43:2 NLT

Why are you downcast, O my soul?
Why so disturbed within me? Put your hope in God,
for I will yet praise him, my Savior and my God.
PSALM 42:11 NIV

Give all your worries and cares to God,
for he cares about you.
1 PETER 5:7 NLT

You will keep him in perfect peace, whose mind
is stayed on You, because he trusts in You.
ISAIAH 26:3 NKJV

Let all that I am wait quietly before God,
for my hope is in him.
PSALM 62:5 NLT

Praise be to the God. . .who comforts us in all our
troubles, so that we can comfort those in any trouble
with the comfort we ourselves have received from God.
For just as the sufferings of Christ flow over into our
lives, so also through Christ our comfort overflows.
2 CORINTHIANS 1:3–5 NIV

May integrity and honesty protect me,
for I put my hope in you.
PSALM 25:21 NLT

Yet what we suffer now is nothing compared
to the glory he will reveal to us later.
ROMANS 8:18 NLT

What's Your Fragrance?

*[God] uses us to spread the knowledge of Christ everywhere,
like a sweet perfume. Our lives are a Christ-like
fragrance rising up to God.*
2 CORINTHIANS 2:14–15 NLT

Did you know that the average human can detect up
to 10,000 different odors? That explains why there
are so many different perfumes at the department store.
Some people prefer musk, while others like something
light and fruity. Some heavy scents can leave us with a
headache, and there are those that stay with us for hours
after the wearer is gone.

Paul says that God gives Christians a fragrance
all their own. When we are kind to someone who
doesn't deserve it, it smells wonderful, a little like grace.
When we help a person in need, our generosity is like
a refreshing fragrance to a weary soul. Forgiveness,
gentleness, self-control—each of these things leaves a
pleasant aroma in the wake of those who share them.
Regardless of what we do, Paul reminds us that our
fragrance should *always* make people think of Christ.

As you live your life today, what kind of fragrance
will you carry with you? Ask God to help you be a
sweet representative of Christ, leaving His delightful
aroma lingering behind you.

*"Don't worry about how to defend yourself or
what to say, for the Holy Spirit will teach
you at that time what needs to be said."*
LUKE 12:11–12 NLT

*Preach the Word; be prepared in season and
out of season; correct, rebuke and encourage—
with great patience and careful instruction.*
2 TIMOTHY 4:2 NIV

*"You're here to be light, bringing out the God-colors
in the world. God is not a secret to be kept. We're going
public with this, as public as a city on a hill. If I make
you light-bearers, you don't think I'm going to hide
you under a bucket, do you? I'm putting you on a light
stand. Now that I've put you there on a hilltop,
on a light stand—shine!"*
MATTHEW 5:14–16 MSG

*But in your hearts set apart Christ as Lord. Always be
prepared to give an answer to everyone who asks you to
give the reason for the hope that you have.*
1 PETER 3:15 NIV

And my speech and my preaching were not
with persuasive words of human wisdom,
but in demonstration of the Spirit and of power,
that your faith should not be in the wisdom
of men but in the power of God.
1 CORINTHIANS 2:4–5 NKJV

Has the LORD redeemed you? Then speak out!
Tell others he has redeemed you from your enemies.
PSALM 107:2 NLT

But God had mercy on me so that Christ Jesus could use
me as a prime example of his great patience with even
the worst sinners. Then others will realize that they,
too, can believe in him and receive eternal life.
1 TIMOTHY 1:16 NLT

So do not be ashamed to testify about our Lord,
or ashamed of me his prisoner. But join with me
in suffering for the gospel, by the power of God,
who has saved us and called us to a holy life—
not because of anything we have done but
because of his own purpose and grace.
2 TIMOTHY 1:8–9 NIV

"I'm sending you off to open the eyes of the outsiders
so they can see the difference between dark and light,
and choose light, see the difference between
Satan and God, and choose God."
ACTS 26:17 MSG

If anyone among you wanders from the truth, and
someone turns him back, let him know that he who
turns a sinner from the error of his way will save a
soul from death and cover a multitude of sins.
JAMES 5:19–20 NKJV

Yet I am not ashamed, because I know whom I have
believed, and am convinced that he is able to guard
what I have entrusted to him for that day. What you
heard from me, keep as the pattern of sound teaching,
with faith and love in Christ Jesus.
2 TIMOTHY 1:12–13 NIV

God's servant must not be argumentative, but a gentle
listener and a teacher who keeps cool, working firmly
but patiently with those who refuse to obey.
2 TIMOTHY 2:25 MSG

Only let your conduct be worthy of the gospel of Christ,
so that whether I come and see you or am absent,
I may hear of your affairs, that you stand fast in one
spirit, with one mind striving together
for the faith of the gospel.
PHILIPPIANS 1:27 NKJV

"Everyone who has left houses or brothers or
sisters or father or mother or wife or children or lands,
for My name's sake, shall receive a hundredfold,
and inherit eternal life."
MATTHEW 19:29 NKJV

But as many as received Him,
to them He gave the right to become children of God,
to those who believe in His name.
JOHN 1:12 NKJV

He will give eternal life to those who keep
on doing good, seeking after the glory and
honor and immortality that God offers.
ROMANS 2:7 NLT

FAILURE

The Morning After

So now there is no condemnation for
those who belong to Christ Jesus.
ROMANS 8:1 NLT

Justin wished for a time machine. He would give
anything to turn back the clock a mere twelve hours.
What seemed like harmless fun last night left a terrible
aftertaste in Justin's mouth this morning—both literally
and figuratively. What was he thinking? And his
fraternity brothers knew he was a Christian, too. What
kind of a witness had he been? Ugh. What a mess.
Justin spent the rest of the day beating himself up. How
would he ever recover from such a failure?

One of the consequences of sin is feeling guilt and
shame for our actions. On one hand, guilt serves an
important purpose—it forces us to come to grips with
the condition of our hearts. But after that, guilt should
point us to Christ so that we can ask for and receive the
forgiveness that is promised to us.

The problem is, many of us get stuck in our
guilt. We begin to feel worthless instead of unworthy,
condemned instead of forgiven. But this is not the truth
that Jesus offers. There is no unforgivable sin and no
action that God cannot redeem. Move past the sin in
your life to a place of healing and forgiveness. It's a gift
God has promised to you that you'll find right at the
foot of the cross.

Blessed is he whose transgression is forgiven,
whose sin is covered.
PSALM 32:1 NKJV

"For I will forgive their wickedness
and will remember their sins no more."
HEBREWS 8:12 NIV

Though we are overwhelmed by our sins,
you forgive them all.
PSALM 65:3 NLT

"No longer will a man teach his neighbor, or a man his
brother, saying, 'Know the LORD,' because they will all
know me, from the least of them to the greatest," declares
the LORD. "For I will forgive their wickedness and will
remember their sins no more."
JEREMIAH 31:34 NIV

If we confess our sins, He is faithful and just to forgive us our sins and to cleanse us from all unrighteousness.
1 John 1:9 NKJV

"Then if my people who are called by my name will humble themselves and pray and seek my face and turn from their wicked ways, I will hear from heaven and will forgive their sins and restore their land."
2 Chronicles 7:14 NLT

"I'll scrub them clean from the dirt they've done against me. I'll forgive everything they've done wrong, forgive all their rebellions."
Jeremiah 33:8 MSG

Bring your confessions, and return to the LORD. Say to him, "Forgive all our sins and graciously receive us, so that we may offer you our praises."
Hosea 14:2 NLT

Seeing then that we have a great High Priest who has passed through the heavens, Jesus the Son of God, let us hold fast our confession. For we do not have a High Priest who cannot sympathize with our weaknesses, but was in all points tempted as we are, yet without sin.
HEBREWS 4:14–15 NKJV

Who then will condemn us? No one—for Christ Jesus died for us and was raised to life for us, and he is sitting in the place of honor at God's right hand, pleading for us.
ROMANS 8:34 NLT

*"Blessed are those who mourn,
for they will be comforted."*
MATTHEW 5:4 NIV

"God didn't go to all the trouble of sending his Son merely to point an accusing finger, telling the world how bad it was. He came to help, to put the world right again."
JOHN 3:17 MSG

"For if you forgive men their trespasses,
your heavenly Father will also forgive you."
MATTHEW 6:14 NKJV

And the result of God's gracious gift is very different
from the result of that one man's sin. For Adam's sin
led to condemnation, but God's free gift leads to
our being made right with God, even though
we are guilty of many sins.
ROMANS 5:16 NLT

If the ministry that condemns men is glorious,
how much more glorious is the ministry
that brings righteousness!
2 CORINTHIANS 3:9 NIV

This then is how we know that we belong to the
truth, and how we set our hearts at rest in his presence
whenever our hearts condemn us. For God is greater
than our hearts, and he knows everything.
1 JOHN 3:19–20 NIV

Owning Your Faith

For you are all children of God through faith in Christ Jesus.
GALATIANS 3:26 NLT

Pattie was raised in a Christian home. She grew up going to church every Sunday and rarely missed a youth group meeting. Her parents prayed with her and taught her to put God first in everything she did. Pattie went away to college knowing her mom and dad expected her to find a church home near her campus.

By the time school started, Pattie had no desire to attend church. For the first few Sunday mornings she slept in, and although she felt guilty, she just couldn't get excited about attending an unfamiliar church.

Things changed when Pattie got involved in a campus fellowship. She started going to a small group and gradually became more excited about living out her faith. Eventually she found a church she loved and looked forward to attending every Sunday. It wasn't necessarily her parents' idea of the perfect church, but it suited Pattie perfectly.

One of the challenges you'll face in this new phase of life is to make your faith your own. Your relationship with God may be shaped by your parents, but the next step for you to become a growing, active, and fruitful Christian is your responsibility. What steps can you take today to make your faith your own?

*"But blessed is the man who trusts me, God,
the woman who sticks with God. They're like trees
replanted in Eden, putting down roots near the
rivers—never a worry through the hottest of summers,
never dropping a leaf, serene and calm through
droughts, bearing fresh fruit every season."*
JEREMIAH 17:7–8 MSG

*Then Jesus told him, "You believe because you have seen
me. Blessed are those who believe without seeing me."*
JOHN 20:29 NLT

*Consequently, faith comes from hearing the message,
and the message is heard through the word of Christ.*
ROMANS 10:17 NIV

"All things are possible to him who believes."
MARK 9:23 NKJV

But without faith it is impossible to please Him, for he who comes to God must believe that He is, and that He is a rewarder of those who diligently seek Him.
HEBREWS 11:6 NKJV

For we are each responsible for our own conduct.
GALATIANS 6:5 NLT

You never saw him, yet you love him. You still don't see him, yet you trust him—with laughter and singing. Because you kept on believing, you'll get what you're looking forward to: total salvation.
1 PETER 1:8–9 MSG

Watch, stand fast in the faith, be brave, be strong.
1 CORINTHIANS 16:13 NKJV

*Now faith is being sure of what we
hope for and certain of what we do not see.*
HEBREWS 11:1 NIV

*For you know that when your faith is tested,
your endurance has a chance to grow. So let it grow, for
when your endurance is fully developed, you will
be perfect and complete, needing nothing.*
JAMES 1:3–4 NLT

*[Jesus] said to the woman,
"Your faith has saved you. Go in peace."*
LUKE 7:50 NKJV

*God's way of putting people right shows up in the acts
of faith, confirming what Scripture has said all along:
"The person in right standing before God
by trusting him really lives."*
ROMANS 1:17 MSG

Let us go right into the presence of God with sincere hearts fully trusting him. For our guilty consciences have been sprinkled with Christ's blood to make us clean, and our bodies have been washed with pure water.
HEBREWS 10:22 NLT

We live by faith, not by sight.
2 CORINTHIANS 5:7 NIV

In addition to all this, take up the shield of faith, with which you can extinguish all the flaming arrows of the evil one.
EPHESIANS 6:16 NIV

The purpose of my instruction is that all believers would be filled with love that comes from a pure heart, a clear conscience, and genuine faith.
1 TIMOTHY 1:5 NLT

The Gift That
Keeps on Giving

∾

*"But when you are praying, first forgive anyone
you are holding a grudge against, so that your
Father in heaven will forgive your sins, too."*
MARK 11:25 NLT

Kim couldn't decide what hurt more: the fact that
her boyfriend broke up with her or the fact that he
was dating someone else while they were together. Not
surprisingly, Kim struggled to forgive her ex-boyfriend.

Friends encouraged her to vent her feelings and
assured her it would help her heal. But even after
months of venting her anger, Kim still didn't feel any
better. In fact, she began to wonder if she was getting
worse.

Maybe you can relate to Kim. Perhaps someone
you once loved has betrayed you beyond what you feel
you can forgive. If you feel this way, know that God
understands. He knows what it feels like to be betrayed
and rejected by us. And yet He forgives us again and
again—a gift that is ours for the asking. Because we
experience His never-ending forgiveness, He asks us
to offer the same gift to others. The truth is, you can't
forgive on your own strength. Ask God for help, and
He'll be there to fill you with a spirit of forgiveness.

"You have heard that it was said, 'Eye for eye, and tooth for tooth.' But I tell you, Do not resist an evil person. If someone strikes you on the right cheek, turn to him the other also."
MATTHEW 5:38–39 NIV

Where is another God like you, who pardons the guilt of the remnant, overlooking the sins of his special people? You will not stay angry with your people forever, because you delight in showing unfailing love.
MICAH 7:18 NLT

Then Peter came to Him and said, "Lord, how often shall my brother sin against me, and I forgive him? Up to seven times?" Jesus said to him, "I do not say to you, up to seven times, but up to seventy times seven."
MATTHEW 18:21–22 NKJV

O my soul, bless GOD, don't forget a single blessing! He forgives your sins—every one. He heals your diseases—every one.
PSALM 103:2–3 MSG

*If we confess our sins, he is faithful and just
and will forgive us our sins and purify
us from all unrighteousness.*
1 JOHN 1:9 NIV

*None of the sins he has committed will be remembered
against him. He has done what is just and right;
he will surely live.*
EZEKIEL 33:16 NIV

*Have mercy on me, O God, because of your
unfailing love. Because of your great compassion,
blot out the stain of my sins.*
PSALM 51:1 NLT

*"This is my blood, God's new covenant poured out
for many people for the forgiveness of sins."*
MATTHEW 26:28 MSG

Instead, be kind to each other, tenderhearted,
forgiving one another, just as God
through Christ has forgiven you.
EPHESIANS 4:32 NLT

"And whenever you stand praying, if you have anything
against anyone, forgive him, that your Father in
heaven may also forgive you your trespasses."
MARK 11:25 NKJV

Don't repay evil for evil. Don't retaliate with
insults when people insult you. Instead, pay them
back with a blessing. That is what God has called
you to do, and he will bless you for it.
1 PETER 3:9 NLT

Smart people know how to hold their tongue;
their grandeur is to forgive and forget.
PROVERBS 19:11 MSG

"If your brother sins against you, rebuke him; and if he repents, forgive him. And if he sins against you seven times in a day, and seven times in a day returns to you, saying, 'I repent,' you shall forgive him."
LUKE 17:3–4 NKJV

"Don't pick on people, jump on their failures, criticize their faults—unless, of course, you want the same treatment. Don't condemn those who are down; that hardness can boomerang. Be easy on people; you'll find life a lot easier."
LUKE 6:37 MSG

Make allowance for each other's faults, and forgive anyone who offends you. Remember, the Lord forgave you, so you must forgive others.
COLOSSIANS 3:13 NLT

Blessed is he whose transgressions are forgiven, whose sins are covered.
PSALM 32:1 NIV

Will Work for Fruit

But the fruit of the Spirit is love, joy, peace, patience,
kindness, goodness, faithfulness, gentleness and self-control.
Against such things there is no law.
GALATIANS 5:22–23 NIV

Have you ever watched apple trees produce apples? It's not exactly exciting. If they receive proper tending and get enough sunlight, water, and nourishment, they bear delicious fruit—no noticeable effort required.

Scripture often uses fruit analogies: We bear the fruit of the Spirit; Jesus prunes branches that don't bear fruit; we recognize other believers by the fruit their lives produce.

Sometimes we incorrectly think that fruit-bearing is a goal we're supposed to achieve—that productive Christians are required to work hard at doing and saying all the right things at all the right times. But working at being patient or kind simply doesn't work.

If you're feeling like you haven't been bearing much fruit lately, take a look at the environment you're planted in. Are you being regularly watered by God's Word? Are you basking in the sunlight of fellowship with other Christians? Are you being routinely nourished by prayer? If these things are a part of your life, soon you'll discover that the fruit you bear is the natural extension of God's love in you.

The mind of sinful man is death, but the mind controlled by the Spirit is life and peace.
ROMANS 8:6 NIV

Peacemakers who sow in peace raise a harvest of righteousness.
JAMES 3:18 NIV

If then you were raised with Christ, seek those things which are above, where Christ is, sitting at the right hand of God. Set your mind on things above, not on things on the earth.
COLOSSIANS 3:1–2 NKJV

Then Abraham waited patiently, and he received what God had promised.
HEBREWS 6:15 NLT

Be humble and gentle. Be patient with each other,
making allowance for each other's
faults because of your love.
EPHESIANS 4:2 NLT

"God is Spirit, and those who worship
Him must worship in spirit and truth."
JOHN 4:24 NKJV

For you know that when your faith is tested,
your endurance has a chance to grow. So let it grow,
for when your endurance is fully developed, you will
be perfect and complete, needing nothing.
JAMES 1:3–4 NLT

But you are not in the flesh but in the Spirit,
if indeed the Spirit of God dwells in you. Now if
anyone does not have the Spirit of Christ, he is not His.
ROMANS 8:9 NKJV

And now I want each of you to extend that same intensity toward a full-bodied hope, and keep at it till the finish. Don't drag your feet. Be like those who stay the course with committed faith and then get everything promised to them.
HEBREWS 6:12 MSG

This calls for patient endurance on the part of the saints who obey God's commandments and remain faithful to Jesus.
REVELATION 14:12 NIV

I have been crucified with Christ; it is no longer I who live, but Christ lives in me; and the life which I now live in the flesh I live by faith in the Son of God, who loved me and gave Himself for me.
GALATIANS 2:20 NKJV

Make every effort to keep yourselves united in the Spirit, binding yourselves together with peace.
EPHESIANS 4:3 NLT

"It will not be you speaking, but the Spirit of your Father speaking through you."
MATTHEW 10:20 NIV

Oh! May the God of green hope fill you up with joy, fill you up with peace, so that your believing lives, filled with the life-giving energy of the Holy Spirit, will brim over with hope!
ROMANS 15:13 MSG

"For the one whom God has sent speaks the words of God, for God gives the Spirit without limit."
JOHN 3:34 NIV

And this hope will not lead to disappointment. For we know how dearly God loves us, because he has given us the Holy Spirit to fill our hearts with his love.
ROMANS 5:5 NLT

The Future

Making Good Decisions

"Choose my instruction instead of silver, knowledge rather than choice gold, for wisdom is more precious than rubies, and nothing you desire can compare with her."
PROVERBS 8:10–11 NIV

Ann felt as if she were about to take the bungee jump of her life—blindfolded. Quitting her secure and well-paying job to pursue her dream of going back to school to become a teacher seemed like the right thing to do, but doubt nagged her.

What if I can't make it financially? What if going back to school is harder than I thought? What if teaching isn't for me? Despite Ann's questions, her heart wouldn't let go of the dream of opening a tutoring center for underprivileged children.

One morning, after a sleepless night of praying for wisdom, the answers seemed clear. She wasn't jumping blindly. She had carefully researched her options. She'd asked for advice from trusted friends. And most importantly, she believed God had prompted her to make this decision.

God's wisdom helps us make good decisions and keeps us from dangerous situations. But sometimes this wisdom seems so difficult to find. How do we really *know* when our plans for the future are part of God's plan? The key is consistency—faithfully seeking God's will, through His Word and through prayer; asking others for advice. Gradually the wise choice becomes clear. God imparts wisdom for the future. It's ours for the asking.

Talk to Wisdom as to a sister.
Treat Insight as your companion.
PROVERBS 7:4 MSG

If you need wisdom, ask our generous God, and he will
give it to you. He will not rebuke you for asking.
JAMES 1:5 NLT

In that day he will be your sure foundation, providing
a rich store of salvation, wisdom, and knowledge.
The fear of the LORD will be your treasure.
ISAIAH 33:6 NLT

For your obedience has become known to all. Therefore
I am glad on your behalf; but I want you to be wise in
what is good, and simple concerning evil.
ROMANS 16:19 NKJV

Those who are wise will shine like the brightness of the heavens, and those who lead many to righteousness, like the stars for ever and ever.
DANIEL 12:3 NIV

If you want to live well, make sure you understand all of this. If you know what's good for you, you'll learn this inside and out. God's paths get you where you want to go. Right-living people walk them easily; wrong-living people are always tripping and stumbling.
HOSEA 14:9 MSG

GOD makes his people strong. GOD gives his people peace.
PSALM 29:11 MSG

Trust in the LORD with all your heart, and lean not on your own understanding.
PROVERBS 3:5 NKJV

*Whoever obeys his command will come to no harm, and
the wise heart will know the proper time and procedure.*
ECCLESIASTES 8:5 NIV

*If you are really wise, you'll think this over—
it's time you appreciated GOD's deep love.*
PSALM 107:43 MSG

*Who is wise and understanding among you?
Let him show by good conduct that his works
are done in the meekness of wisdom.*
JAMES 3:13 NKJV

*"Therefore everyone who hears these words of mine and
puts them into practice is like a wise man who built his
house on the rock. The rain came down, the streams rose,
and the winds blew and beat against that house; yet it
did not fall, because it had its foundation on the rock."*
MATTHEW 7:24–25 NIV

We speak of God's secret wisdom,
a wisdom that has been hidden and that God
destined for our glory before time began.
1 CORINTHIANS 2:7 NIV

How much better to get wisdom than gold! And to get
understanding is to be chosen rather than silver.
PROVERBS 16:16 NKJV

The LORD of Heaven's Armies is a wonderful teacher,
and he gives the farmer great wisdom.
ISAIAH 28:29 NLT

Let the wise listen to these proverbs and become even
wiser. Let those with understanding receive guidance.
PROVERBS 1:5 NLT

GIVING

God First

"Give, and you will receive. Your gift will return to you in full—pressed down, shaken together to make room for more, running over, and poured into your lap. The amount you give will determine the amount you get back."
LUKE 6:38 NLT

After four hard years of college, Greg landed his dream job and finally made enough money to live on his own. As he sat down with his dad to review his budget, he was proud to show that there was enough to cover rent, insurance, and even a little spending money.

"What about your tithe?" Greg's dad asked.

"Well, uh. . .I guess I was just thinking I'd wait until I made a little more money. . . ." Greg stumbled.

"Over the years I've learned to set aside my tithe before paying for anything else," his dad said. "As a result, I've discovered that God is always faithful to meet my needs—and more. Don't sell yourself short, Greg. You can swing it."

Greg decided to follow his dad's advice, and amazingly, he had more than enough money to meet his needs.

God's economy is different than the world's. The principle is to give a portion of what God has already blessed you with. In return He promises to meet your every need and more. As you embark on a new stage of life, start putting God first in your finances. You won't regret it.

A good name is to be chosen rather than great riches,
loving favor rather than silver and gold.
PROVERBS 22:1 NKJV

But remember the LORD your God, for it is
he who gives you the ability to produce wealth,
and so confirms his covenant, which he swore
to your forefathers, as it is today.
DEUTERONOMY 8:18 NIV

Honor the LORD with your wealth and with
the best part of everything you produce. Then
he will fill your barns with grain, and your
vats will overflow with good wine.
PROVERBS 3:9–10 NLT

Don't be obsessed with getting more material things. Be
relaxed with what you have. Since God assured us, "I'll
never let you down, never walk off and leave you."
HEBREWS 13:5 MSG

Those who desire to be rich fall into temptation and a snare, and into many foolish and harmful lusts which drown men in destruction and perdition. For the love of money is a root of all kinds of evil, for which some have strayed from the faith in their greediness, and pierced themselves through with many sorrows.
1 TIMOTHY 6:9–11 NKJV

Every man shall give as he is able, according to the blessing of the LORD your God which He has given you.
DEUTERONOMY 16:17 NKJV

"Here's the lesson: Use your worldly resources to benefit others and make friends. Then, when your earthly possessions are gone, they will welcome you to an eternal home."
LUKE 16:9 NLT

Trust in your money and down you go! But the godly flourish like leaves in spring.
PROVERBS 11:28 NLT

"You can't worship two gods at once. Loving one god, you'll end up hating the other. Adoration of one feeds contempt for the other. You can't worship God and Money both."
MATTHEW 6:24 MSG

I have seen a grievous evil under the sun: wealth hoarded to the harm of its owner, or wealth lost through some misfortune, so that when he has a son there is nothing left for him. Naked a man comes from his mother's womb, and as he comes, so he departs.
ECCLESIASTES 5:13–15 NIV

Command those who are rich in this present world not to be arrogant nor to put their hope in wealth, which is so uncertain, but to put their hope in God, who richly provides us with everything for our enjoyment.
1 TIMOTHY 6:17 NIV

So let each one give as he purposes in his heart, not grudgingly or of necessity; for God loves a cheerful giver.
2 CORINTHIANS 9:7 NKJV

Speaking to the people, [Jesus] went on, "Take care!
Protect yourself against the least bit of greed. Life is not
defined by what you have, even when you have a lot."
LUKE 12:15 MSG

Believers who are poor have something to boast about,
for God has honored them. And those who are rich
should boast that God has humbled them.
JAMES 1:9–10 NLT

"Do not store up for yourselves treasures on earth, where
moth and rust destroy, and where thieves break in and
steal. But store up for yourselves treasures in heaven. . . .
For where your treasure is, there your heart will be also."
MATTHEW 6:19–21 NIV

Since we entered the world penniless and
will leave it penniless, if we have bread on
the table and shoes on our feet, that's enough.
1 TIMOTHY 6:7–8 MSG

GOD'S LOVE

Searching for Love

*"As the Father has loved me, so have I loved you.
Now remain in my love."*
JOHN 15:9 NIV

The perfect fairy-tale wedding has always been Krista's dream. She imagines herself adorned in a snow-white dress walking down the aisle, awash with rose petals. She is confident that if she waits long enough and patiently enough, her Prince Charming will come to give her the love she's always dreamed of.

What Krista doesn't know is that her future husband will never be able to love her just in the way she longs for. No spouse can. Many couples enter marriage believing that it's the beginning of an effortless happily-ever-after. They look to one another to fulfill their every need. It doesn't take long for disappointment and disillusionment to set in when their spouses fail to meet their expectations. These expectations are for a perfect love, and the truth is, no human being can love us the way God created us to be loved.

Only God can fill the void in our hearts. When we learn to allow God's love to seep into our deepest places and fill our deepest needs, our human relationships are transformed. Instead of holding others to high and impossible expectations, we are free to receive the love that they can offer us without being selfish and demanding, because we are allowing God to meet our deepest love needs.

"For God loved the world so much that he gave his one and only Son, so that everyone who believes in him will not perish but have eternal life."
JOHN 3:16 NLT

Await the mercy of our Lord Jesus Christ, who will bring you eternal life. In this way, you will keep yourselves safe in God's love.
JUDE 1:21 NLT

The LORD says, "Then I will heal you of your faithlessness; my love will know no bounds, for my anger will be gone forever."
HOSEA 14:4 NLT

And I ask him that with both feet planted firmly on love, you'll be able to take in with all followers of Jesus the extravagant dimensions of Christ's love. Reach out and experience the breadth! Test its length! Plumb the depths! Rise to the heights! Live full lives, full in the fullness of God.
EPHESIANS 3:17 MSG

For I am convinced that neither death nor life, neither angels nor demons, neither the present nor the future, nor any powers, neither height nor depth, nor anything else in all creation, will be able to separate us from the love of God that is in Christ Jesus our Lord.
ROMANS 8:38–39 NIV

"I'll be with you as you do this, day after day after day, right up to the end of the age."
MATTHEW 28:20 MSG

GOD, your God, is above all a compassionate God. In the end he will not abandon you, he won't bring you to ruin, he won't forget the covenant with your ancestors which he swore to them.
DEUTERONOMY 4:31 MSG

And hope does not disappoint us, because God has poured out his love into our hearts by the Holy Spirit, whom he has given us.
ROMANS 5:5 NIV

And we have known and believed the love that
God has for us. God is love, and he who abides
in love abides in God, and God in him.
1 JOHN 4:16 NKJV

But you, O God, are both tender and kind, not easily
angered, immense in love, and you never, never quit.
PSALM 86:15 MSG

But God demonstrates his own love for us in this:
While we were still sinners, Christ died for us.
ROMANS 5:8 NIV

What marvelous love the Father has extended to us!
Just look at it—we're called children of God!
That's who we really are.
1 JOHN 3:1 MSG

*The LORD passed in front of Moses, calling out,
"Yahweh! The LORD! The God of compassion
and mercy! I am slow to anger and filled with
unfailing love and faithfulness."*
EXODUS 34:6 NLT

*He fulfills the desires of those who fear him;
he hears their cry and saves them.
The LORD watches over all who love him.*
PSALM 145:19–20 NIV

*God showed how much he loved us by sending his
one and only Son into the world so that we might
have eternal life through him. This is real love—
not that we loved God, but that he loved us and
sent his Son as a sacrifice to take away our sins.*
1 JOHN 4:9–10 NLT

*"The Father Himself loves you, because you have loved
Me, and have believed that I came forth from God."*
JOHN 16:27 NKJV

GOD'S PROVISION

Daily Bread

⚬

"Give us today our daily bread."
MATTHEW 6:11 NIV

Most of us don't really know what it means to rely on God for our daily bread. Our kitchen shelves are usually well-stocked with food—enough to carry us well through the week if not through a month or two. Even when we feel like there's "nothing to eat in the house" we could probably rustle up a pretty decent meal with a little bit of effort. Yet in the book of Matthew, Jesus teaches us to pray for our daily bread.

The Israelites would have had a much clearer understanding of the concept of daily bread. In Exodus 16, when they complained of their discomfort and hunger in the desert, God explained that he would "rain down bread from heaven" (Exodus 16:4). The people were instructed to only gather what they would need for the day—anything more would spoil. Those who didn't follow God's instructions and tried to save some for the next morning ended up with a tent full of maggots. There are three principles we can learn from this story.

1. We can trust God to provide for our daily needs.
2. God's provision is enough—it is not necessary to hoard his blessings.
3. Relying on his provision frees us to think about other, more important, things.

God promises to provide your daily bread. You can trust him to do it.

*"But the very hairs of your head are all numbered.
Do not fear therefore; you are of more
value than many sparrows."*
LUKE 12:7 NKJV

*Whatever is good and perfect comes down to us from God
our Father, who created all the lights in the heavens.
He never changes or casts a shifting shadow. He chose to
give birth to us by giving us his true word. And we,
out of all creation, became his prized possession.*
JAMES 1:17–18 NLT

*And the house of Israel called its name Manna.
And it was like white coriander seed, and the
taste of it was like wafers made with honey.*
EXODUS 16:31 NKJV

*Those who know your name will trust in you, for you,
LORD, have never forsaken those who seek you.*
PSALM 9:10 NIV

And my God will meet all your needs according to his glorious riches in Christ Jesus.
PHILIPPIANS 4:19 NIV

"What I'm trying to do here is to get you to relax, to not be so preoccupied with getting, so you can respond to God's giving. People who don't know God and the way he works fuss over these things, but you know both God and how he works. Steep your life in God-reality, God-initiative, God-provisions. Don't worry about missing out. You'll find all your everyday human concerns will be met."
MATTHEW 6:31–33 MSG

[GOD] guards you when you leave and when you return, he guards you now, he guards you always.
PSALM 121:8 MSG

Abraham named the place Yahweh-Yireh (which means "the LORD will provide"). To this day, people still use that name as a proverb: "On the mountain of the LORD it will be provided."
GENESIS 22:14 NLT

And my God shall supply all your need according
to His riches in glory by Christ Jesus.
PHILIPPIANS 4:19 NKJV

Those who seek the LORD
shall not lack any good thing.
PSALM 34:10 NKJV

Keep falsehood and lies far from me; give me neither
poverty nor riches, but give me only my daily bread.
PROVERBS 30:8 NIV

He gave food to those who fear him,
He remembered to keep his ancient promise.
PSALM 111:5 MSG

"Your Father knows what you need before you ask him."
MATTHEW 6:8 NIV

He rained down showers of manna to eat,
he gave them the Bread of Heaven.
PSALM 78:24 MSG

You sent your good Spirit to instruct them,
and you did not stop giving them manna
from heaven or water for their thirst.
NEHEMIAH 9:20 NLT

"And don't be concerned about what to eat and
what to drink. Don't worry about such things."
LUKE 12:29 NLT

GRATITUDE

Plan B

Be thankful in all circumstances, for this is
God's will for you who belong to Christ Jesus.
1 THESSALONIANS 5:18 NLT

Sara was head cheerleader in high school and was known for her perkiness and optimism. So when she tried out for her college's cheer squad, she did so with the utmost confidence. When the tryout results were posted, Sara couldn't believe her name wasn't listed. She was deeply disappointed as she tried to imagine surviving a whole football season without cheerleading. Then her roommate suggested Sara join her on Wednesday afternoons when she volunteered as a reading tutor at a local community center. Why not? It wasn't like she had anything better to do.

By the end of the school year, Sara wouldn't have missed those Wednesday afternoons for anything. She grew to love the children in a way she never would have imagined and ended up changing her major to elementary education. As she looked back, Sara found herself extremely grateful she hadn't made the cheerleading squad—or she might never have taken the opportunity to experience such a rewarding activity.

When our plans don't work out, gratitude is not always the first feeling that comes to mind. We might first feel frustrated, angry, disappointed, or humiliated. But the next time Plan A doesn't work, try being grateful and wait to see what God will do. More often than not, God's Plan B is more wonderful than we could ever dream.

Let me shout God's name with a praising song,
let me tell his greatness in a prayer of thanks.
PSALM 69:30 MSG

Give thanks for everything to God the
Father in the name of our Lord Jesus Christ.
EPHESIANS 5:20 NLT

In everything give thanks;
for this is the will of God in Christ Jesus for you.
1 THESSALONIANS 5:18 NKJV

But thanks be to God, who gives us the
victory through our Lord Jesus Christ.
1 CORINTHIANS 15:57 NKJV

Then he took the seven loaves and the fish, and when he had given thanks, he broke them and gave them to the disciples, and they in turn to the people.
MATTHEW 15:36 NIV

And whatever you do or say, do it as a representative of the Lord Jesus, giving thanks through him to God the Father.
COLOSSIANS 3:17 NLT

Let us come before His presence with thanksgiving; let us shout joyfully to Him with psalms.
PSALM 95:2 NKJV

In that wonderful day you will sing: "Thank the LORD! Praise his name! Tell the nations what he has done. Let them know how mighty he is!"
ISAIAH 12:4 NLT

Give thanks to GOD—
he is good and his love never quits.
1 CHRONICLES 16:34 MSG

Are any of you suffering hardships? You should pray.
Are any of you happy? You should sing praises.
JAMES 5:13 NLT

I will praise You, O LORD, with my whole heart;
I will tell of all Your marvelous works.
PSALM 9:1 NKJV

"But I, with a song of thanksgiving, will sacrifice
to you. What I have vowed I will make good.
Salvation comes from the LORD."
JONAH 2:9 NIV

Do not be anxious about anything, but in everything,
by prayer and petition, with thanksgiving,
present your requests to God.
PHILIPPIANS 4:6 NIV

I urge, then, first of all, that requests, prayers,
intercession and thanksgiving be made for everyone.
1 TIMOTHY 2:1 NIV

For all things are for your sakes, that grace,
having spread through the many, may cause
thanksgiving to abound to the glory of God.
2 CORINTHIANS 4:15 NKJV

Sing to GOD a thanksgiving hymn,
play music on your instruments to God.
PSALM 147:7 MSG

True Friend

A friend loves at all times.
PROVERBS 17:17 NIV

Katie sighed as she hung up the phone. It was her friend Christine—for the third time that week.

"I hope I'm not bothering you. . . ." Christine began. "I *have* to talk to someone, and you always give such great advice. You don't mind do you?"

Katie hesitated. In truth, Christine's constant phone calls were really starting to irritate her. But even though Christine was insensitive about interrupting and those phone calls often took up more than an hour, Katie didn't have the heart to tell her the truth. Instead she said, "Sure—I've got all the time you need." By the time the conversation was over, Katie's frustration was at an all-time high and once again Christine didn't have a clue. Katie wished there was a way to let Christine know how she felt without losing the friendship, but she wasn't sure how to do it.

Telling the truth is often accompanied by consequences. When we are truthful with others, it can sometimes mean hurting their feelings or changing the relationship. But the Bible is clear—when we fail to speak the truth in love, we are failing to live authentic lives and ultimately can do real damage to ourselves and others. Is there someone in your life with whom you are having difficulty telling the truth? What steps can you take today to be more truthful?

Be completely humble and gentle;
be patient, bearing with one another in love.
EPHESIANS 4:2 NIV

But you desire honesty from the womb,
teaching me wisdom even there.
PSALM 51:6 NLT

The end of a thing is better than its beginning;
the patient in spirit is better than the proud in spirit.
ECCLESIASTES 7:8 NKJV

We reject all shameful deeds and underhanded methods.
We don't try to trick anyone or distort the word
of God. We tell the truth before God,
and all who are honest know this.
2 CORINTHIANS 4:2 NLT

*Pray for us, for our conscience is clear and we
want to live honorably in everything we do.*
HEBREWS 13:18 NLT

*God can't stomach liars;
he loves the company of those who keep their word.*
PROVERBS 12:22 MSG

*Let integrity and uprightness preserve me,
for I wait for You.*
PSALM 25:21 NKJV

*"Here is a simple, rule-of-thumb guide for behavior:
Ask yourself what you want people to do for you, then
grab the initiative and do it for them. Add up God's
Law and Prophets and this is what you get."*
MATTHEW 7:12 MSG

An honest answer is like a warm hug.
PROVERBS 24:26 MSG

*We are taking pains to do what is right,
not only in the eyes of the Lord but
also in the eyes of men.*
2 CORINTHIANS 8:21 NIV

"Do not lie. Do not deceive one another."
LEVITICUS 19:11 NIV

*The LORD detests the use of dishonest scales,
but he delights in accurate weights.*
PROVERBS 11:1 NLT

*Do not lie to each other, since you have taken
off your old self with its practices and have put
on the new self, which is being renewed in
knowledge in the image of its Creator.*
COLOSSIANS 3:9–10 NIV

*Mark the blameless man, and observe the upright;
for the future of that man is peace.*
PSALM 37:37 NKJV

*He who speaks truth declares righteousness,
but a false witness, deceit.*
PROVERBS 12:17 NKJV

*Buy truth—don't sell it for love or money;
buy wisdom, buy education, buy insight.*
PROVERBS 23:23 MSG

HOPE

Light

〜

You are my lamp, O LORD;
the LORD turns my darkness into light.
2 SAMUEL 22:29 NIV

The Bible begins with light. Genesis 1:3 NIV tells us, "And God said, 'Let there be light,' and there was light." It also ends with light. Revelation 22:5 NIV says, "There will be no more night. They will not need the light of a lamp or the light of the sun, for the Lord God will give them light."

Unfortunately, there's a lot of darkness in between. War. Murder. Pain. Loss. But even in the midst of the darkness there are glorious glimpses of His marvelous light. David's sin is forgiven and he becomes a man after God's own heart. Paul is transformed from a murderer of Christians to a passionate evangelist. Peter denied Christ, but that wasn't his destiny—instead he defends Christ to the death. God has the amazing ability to turn even our darkest situations into personal and spiritual victories.

Perhaps you are facing a dark situation right now. Maybe you've suffered loss, a moral failure, or missed a chance to defend your faith. If so, you're not alone. When it seems that you're surrounded by darkness, remember that light is both your foundation and your future. Release the situation to His marvelous light and know that He is able to transform it into something beautiful and worthwhile.

"For You are my lamp, O LORD;
the LORD shall enlighten my darkness."
2 SAMUEL 22:29 NKJV

"The people who sat in darkness have seen a great light.
And for those who lived in the land where death
casts its shadow, a light has shined."
MATTHEW 4:16 NLT

The LORD is my light and my salvation;
whom shall I fear? The LORD is the strength of my life;
of whom shall I be afraid?
PSALM 27:1 NKJV

"He uncovers mysteries hidden in darkness;
he brings light to the deepest gloom."
JOB 12:22 NLT

Send out your light and your truth; let them guide me.
Let them lead me to your holy mountain,
to the place where you live.
PSALM 43:3 NLT

But if we walk in the light, as he is in the light,
we have fellowship with one another, and the
blood of Jesus, his Son, purifies us from all sin.
1 JOHN 1:7 NIV

His brightness was like the light; He had rays flashing
from His hand, and there His power was hidden.
HABAKKUK 3:4 NKJV

"For as long as I am in the world,
there is plenty of light. I am the world's Light."
JOHN 9:5 MSG

*For the LORD God is a sun and shield; the LORD will
give grace and glory; no good thing will He withhold
from those who walk uprightly.*
PSALM 84:11 NKJV

In him was life, and that life was the light of men.
JOHN 1:4 NIV

Let the light of your face shine upon us, O LORD.
PSALM 4:6 NIV

*Oh, how sweet the light of day,
and how wonderful to live in the sunshine!*
ECCLESIASTES 11:7 MSG

The City doesn't need sun or moon for light.
God's Glory is its light, the Lamb its lamp!
REVELATION 21:23 MSG

God said, "Light up the darkness!" and our lives
filled up with light as we saw and understood God in
the face of Christ, all bright and beautiful.
2 CORINTHIANS 4:6 MSG

But you are not like that, for you are a chosen people.
You are royal priests, a holy nation, God's very own
possession. As a result, you can show others the goodness
of God, for he called you out of the darkness
into his wonderful light.
1 PETER 2:9 NLT

The precepts of the LORD are right, giving
joy to the heart. The commands of the LORD
are radiant, giving light to the eyes.
PSALM 19:8 NIV

What's the Secret?

I know what it is to be in need, and I know what it
is to have plenty. I have learned the secret of being
content in any and every situation, whether well fed
or hungry, whether living in plenty or in want.
PHILIPPIANS 4:12 NIV

Since Paul traveled extensively throughout the
Mediterranean, he could have easily penned
Philippians 4:12 from a tranquil seaside villa. The truth
is that he was confined to a dark and lifeless prison cell
when he wrote it. It's one thing to be content when
we're basking in the sun, quite another thing when life
is falling apart at the seams.

The secret to contentment and joy, as Paul
discovered, is twofold. One is to realize that even good
situations can change on a dime. One day you can be
sailing on clear blue waters and the next day be tossed
about in the perfect storm. We are wise to remember
that our circumstances—good or bad—will not last
forever.

The second part is knowing you're never alone.
Although human strength doesn't travel from calm to
turbulent waters very smoothly, the One who walked
on water is quite comfortable in the storm. He'll never
leave you.

Decide to find joy and contentment in Jesus today.

The LORD is my strength and my shield; my heart trusted in Him, and I am helped; therefore my heart greatly rejoices, and with my song I will praise Him.
PSALM 28:7 NKJV

You will go out in joy and be led forth in peace; the mountains and hills will burst into song before you, and all the trees of the field will clap their hands.
ISAIAH 55:12 NIV

Be joyful in hope, patient in affliction, faithful in prayer.
ROMANS 12:12 NIV

"You have made known to me the ways of life; You will make me full of joy in Your presence."
ACTS 2:28 NKJV

Those who plant in tears will harvest with shouts of joy. They weep as they go to plant their seed, but they sing as they return with the harvest.
PSALM 126:5–6 NLT

"I have told you these things so that you will be filled with my joy. Yes, your joy will overflow!"
JOHN 15:11 NLT

God will let you laugh again; you'll raise the roof with shouts of joy.
JOB 8:21 MSG

But let all who take refuge in you rejoice; let them sing joyful praises forever. Spread your protection over them, that all who love your name may be filled with joy.
PSALM 5:11 NLT

I will sing for joy in God, explode in praise from deep in my soul! He dressed me up in a suit of salvation, he outfitted me in a robe of righteousness, as a bridegroom who puts on a tuxedo and a bride a jeweled tiara.
ISAIAH 61:10 MSG

You will show me the way of life, granting me the joy of your presence and the pleasures of living with you forever.
PSALM 16:11 NLT

"But now I come to You, and these things I speak in the world, that they may have My joy fulfilled in themselves."
JOHN 17:13 NKJV

Rejoice in the Lord always. Again I will say, rejoice!
PHILIPPIANS 4:4 NKJV

*In the same way God's ransomed will come back, come
back to Zion cheering, shouting, joy eternal wreathing
their heads, exuberant ecstasies transporting them—
and not a sign of moans or groans.*
ISAIAH 51:11 MSG

*A cheerful heart is good medicine,
but a crushed spirit dries up the bones.*
PROVERBS 17:22 NIV

*But rejoice that you participate in the
sufferings of Christ, so that you may be
overjoyed when his glory is revealed.*
1 PETER 4:13 NIV

*Consider it a sheer gift, friends, when tests and
challenges come at you from all sides. You know
that under pressure, your faith-life is forced
into the open and shows its true colors.*
JAMES 1:2 MSG

JUSTICE

One Life

Share each other's burdens,
and in this way obey the law of Christ.
GALATIANS 6:2 NLT

Emily had recently taken a greater interest in social justice issues and now was feeling overwhelmed. Hunger, poverty, war. . .the more she read and became aware about what was going on in the world, the more depressed and sad she became. She desperately wanted to help everyone who needed it, but nothing she did seemed to even make a dent in this enormous problem.

Many people today look at the seemingly dismal conditions of our world and become paralyzed by the enormity of it all. Some become so intimidated they end up doing nothing at all. It's important to remember that it's not our responsibility to solve the whole world's problems. Instead of becoming overwhelmed to the point of paralysis, we can be far more productive when we simply focus our energies on the people God brings across our paths each day.

Look around you. What needs do the people in your life have? Perhaps there's a local food pantry or homeless shelter where you can volunteer. Maybe there's a person on the subway or bus you ride that could use a listening ear. Making a small difference in the life of one person may not change the world, but it can make all the difference in the world to that one person.

The good-hearted understand what it's like to be poor;
the hardhearted haven't the faintest idea.
PROVERBS 29:7 MSG

Say no to wrong. Learn to do good. Work for justice.
Help the down-and-out. Stand up for the homeless.
Go to bat for the defenseless.
ISAIAH 1:17 MSG

The LORD is a shelter for the oppressed, a refuge in times
of trouble. Those who know your name trust in you, for
you, O LORD, do not abandon those who search for you.
PSALM 9:9–10 NLT

But the needy will not always be forgotten,
nor the hope of the afflicted ever perish.
PSALM 9:18 NIV

*"Don't pervert justice. Don't show favoritism
to either the poor or the great. Judge on
the basis of what is right."*
LEVITICUS 19:15 MSG

*"Stop judging by mere appearances,
and make a right judgment."*
JOHN 7:24 NIV

*Do not pervert justice or show partiality. Do not accept
a bribe, for a bribe blinds the eyes of the wise and twists
the words of the righteous. Follow justice and justice
alone, so that you may live and possess the land the
LORD your God is giving you.*
DEUTERONOMY 16:19–20 NIV

*He shall bring forth your righteousness as the light,
and your justice as the noonday.*
PSALM 37:6 NKJV

God has called us to live holy lives, not impure lives.
Therefore, anyone who refuses to live by these rules
is not disobeying human teaching but is rejecting
God, who gives his Holy Spirit to you.
1 THESSALONIANS 4:7–8 NLT

This is what the LORD says: Be fair-minded and just.
Do what is right! Help those who have been robbed;
rescue them from their oppressors. Quit your evil deeds!
Do not mistreat foreigners, orphans, and widows.
Stop murdering the innocent!
JEREMIAH 22:3 NLT

This is what the LORD says: "Be just and fair to all. Do
what is right and good, for I am coming soon to rescue
you and to display my righteousness among you."
ISAIAH 56:1 NLT

Hate evil, love good; establish justice in the gate.
It may be that the LORD God of hosts will be gracious.
AMOS 5:15 NKJV

Good people celebrate when justice triumphs,
but for the workers of evil it's a bad day.
PROVERBS 21:15 MSG

Thus says the LORD of hosts: 'Execute true justice,
show mercy and compassion everyone to his brother.'"
ZECHARIAH 7:9 NKJV

Yet the LORD longs to be gracious to you; he rises to
show you compassion. For the LORD is a God of justice.
Blessed are all who wait for him!
ISAIAH 30:18 NIV

He has shown you, O man, what is good; and what does
the LORD require of you but to do justly, to love mercy,
and to walk humbly with your God?
MICAH 6:8 NKJV

OBEDIENCE

Choose Wisely

Here now is my final conclusion: Fear God and obey his commands, for this is everyone's duty.
ECCLESIASTES 12:13 NLT

The plan was simple and, from Joe's perspective, extremely economical. The term paper was due the week after Spring Break. Joe wanted to go skiing, so he decided to hire someone to write the paper for him.

He tried to talk Mike into doing the same. "There's no way you can go skiing and get the term paper done, so do it my way and you can have the best of both worlds." There was only one problem. Joe's plan was wrong and Mike knew it. In the end he decided to skip the ski trip and write his own paper. As far as he knew, Joe never got caught, but Mike was glad he could turn the paper in with a clear conscience, even if it did mean missing a week of skiing.

Choosing obedience sometimes means making a hard choice. Sometimes it's merely the sacrifice of convenience or comfort, but often the stakes are higher. Paul was obedient and it landed him in prison. Philippians 2 tells us that Jesus was obedient—to the point of death. You may not always be immediately rewarded for your obedience. But when you make choices that honor God, you can be sure that even if no one else notices, He is nodding His head with loving approval.

"If you keep My commandments, you will abide in My love, just as I have kept My Father's commandments and abide in His love."
JOHN 15:10 NKJV

Whatever you have learned or received or heard from me, or seen in me—put it into practice. And the God of peace will be with you.
PHILIPPIANS 4:9 NIV

"What is more pleasing to the LORD: your burnt offerings and sacrifices or your obedience to his voice? Listen! Obedience is better than sacrifice."
1 SAMUEL 15:22 NLT

"If they obey and serve him, they'll have a good, long life on easy street. But if they disobey, they'll be cut down in their prime and never know the first thing about life."
JOB 36:11 MSG

For the person who keeps all of the laws except one is as guilty as a person who has broken all of God's laws.
JAMES 2:10 NLT

If you are willing and obedient, you shall eat the good of the land.
ISAIAH 1:19 NKJV

"Knowing the correct password—saying 'Master, Master,' for instance—isn't going to get you anywhere with me. What is required is serious obedience— doing what my Father wills."
MATTHEW 7:21 MSG

Obey your spiritual leaders, and do what they say. Their work is to watch over your souls, and they are accountable to God. Give them reason to do this with joy and not with sorrow. That would certainly not be for your benefit.
HEBREWS 13:17 NLT

The LORD leads with unfailing love and faithfulness all who keep his covenant and obey his demands.
PSALM 25:10 NLT

We know that we have come to know him if we obey his commands. . . . But if anyone obeys his word, God's love is truly made complete in him. This is how we know we are in him: Whoever claims to live in him must walk as Jesus did.
1 JOHN 2:3, 5–6 NIV

Oh, that they had such a heart in them that they would fear Me and always keep all My commandments, that it might be well with them and with their children forever!
DEUTERONOMY 5:29 NKJV

My son, do not forget my law, but let your heart keep my commands; for length of days and long life and peace they will add to you.
PROVERBS 3:1–2 NKJV

Merely hearing God's law is a waste of your time if you
don't do what he commands. Doing, not hearing,
is what makes the difference with God.
ROMANS 2:13 MSG

The world and all its wanting, wanting,
wanting is on the way out—but whoever
does what God wants is set for eternity.
1 JOHN 2:17 MSG

"Blessed rather are those who hear
the word of God and obey it."
LUKE 11:28 NIV

I command you today to love the LORD your God,
to walk in his ways, and to keep his commands,
decrees and laws; then you will live and increase,
and the LORD your God will bless you in the
land you are entering to possess.
DEUTERONOMY 30:16 NIV

PEACE

Perfect Peace

You will keep in perfect peace all who trust in you,
all whose thoughts are fixed on you!
ISAIAH 26:3 NLT

Suzanne was exhausted. Pressures at work had become increasingly intense and each day she felt as if she was falling further and further behind. She desperately tried to pray about her situation, but after a while, the words just wouldn't come. She became so consumed by the details of her demanding job, she didn't know where to begin. She tossed and turned at night, wondering how she was going to get it all done.

Have you ever felt this way? Jesus understands that life can be busy and overwhelming. He knows that it sometimes seems like too much to bear. His advice in this regard is simple: Do not worry about tomorrow; each day has enough trouble of its own. Looking too far ahead into the future—even one day—can paralyze us with worry and exhaustion, so much so that we don't feel like doing anything at all.

Jesus taught that it's far more effective to tackle life one step at a time. Not only does this keep our worry at a minimum, it enables us to trust God to help us accomplish what we cannot do on our own. Living in the moment takes practice, but it's a worthwhile investment of your time.

I will lie down and sleep in peace, for you alone,
O LORD, make me dwell in safety.
PSALM 4:8 NIV

Now may the Lord of peace Himself give you peace
always in every way. The Lord be with you all.
2 THESSALONIANS 3:16 NKJV

And let the peace of God rule in your hearts, to which
also you were called in one body; and be thankful.
COLOSSIANS 3:15 NKJV

But all who listen to me will live in peace,
untroubled by fear of harm.
PROVERBS 1:33 NLT

Behold, I will bring it health and healing;
I will heal them and reveal to them
the abundance of peace and truth.
JEREMIAH 33:6 NKJV

Don't worry about anything; instead,
pray about everything. Tell God what you need,
and thank him for all he has done. Then you will
experience God's peace, which exceeds anything we
can understand. His peace will guard your hearts
and minds as you live in Christ Jesus.
PHILIPPIANS 4:6–7 NLT

"Peace I leave with you; my peace I give you.
I do not give to you as the world gives. Do not
let your hearts be troubled and do not be afraid."
JOHN 14:27 NIV

I waited patiently for the LORD to help me,
and he turned to me and heard my cry.
PSALM 40:1 NLT

"Glory to God in the highest, and on earth peace,
goodwill toward men!"
LUKE 2:14 NKJV

May the God of hope fill you with all joy and
peace as you trust in him, so that you may overflow
with hope by the power of the Holy Spirit.
ROMANS 15:13 NIV

"I'll make a covenant of peace with them that will
hold everything together, an everlasting covenant."
EZEKIEL 37:26 MSG

God doesn't stir us up into confusion;
he brings us into harmony.
1 CORINTHIANS 14:33 MSG

"For even if the mountains walk away and the hills fall to pieces, my love won't walk away from you, my covenant commitment of peace won't fall apart." The God who has compassion on you says so.
ISAIAH 54:10 MSG

"These things I have spoken to you, that in Me you may have peace. In the world you will have tribulation; but be of good cheer, I have overcome the world."
JOHN 16:33 NKJV

Letting your sinful nature control your mind leads to death. But letting the Spirit control your mind leads to life and peace.
ROMANS 8:6 NLT

*GOD makes his people strong.
GOD gives his people peace.*
PSALM 29:11 MSG

The Waiting Game

*The LORD kept his word and did for Sarah exactly what
he had promised. She became pregnant, and she gave birth
to a son for Abraham in his old age. This happened at
just the time God had said it would.*
GENESIS 21:1–2 NLT

In Genesis 15 God told Abraham—an old and
childless man—that he would have so many
descendants he would never be able to count them all.

Instead of waiting on God, Abraham's wife, Sarah,
decided to take matters into her own hands by offering
her maidservant, Hagar, to Abraham. This relationship
resulted in the birth of Ishmael. You can imagine the
problems this caused between the two women.

Later, when she was blessed with her own son,
Isaac, Sarah must have wondered why she didn't simply
wait for God's plan to be fulfilled. His plan was *so* much
better than hers.

Have you ever prayed for something, then told
God how to make it happen? When we take matters
into our own hands, we're limiting God's work in our
lives. What are you waiting for today? Are you waiting
to hear about a job offer or acceptance to the school of
your choice? Wondering if your long-term relationship
will turn into marriage? Whatever your need, give it to
God. Relax and let Him handle it for you. The results
will be better than you could ever dream.

*"This calls for patient endurance on
the part of the saints who obey God's
commandments and remain faithful to Jesus.*
REVELATION 14:12 NIV

*We can rejoice, too, when we run into problems and
trials, for we know that they help us develop endurance.
And endurance develops strength of character, and
character strengthens our confident hope of salvation.*
ROMANS 5:3–4 NLT

*Let us hold fast the confession of our hope without
wavering, for He who promised is faithful.*
HEBREWS 10:23 NKJV

*Now may the Lord direct your hearts into
the love of God and into the patience of Christ.*
2 THESSALONIANS 3:5 NKJV

So let's not allow ourselves to get fatigued doing good.
At the right time we will harvest a good
crop if we don't give up, or quit.
GALATIANS 6:9 MSG

To him who overcomes I will grant to sit with
Me on My throne, as I also overcame and sat down
with My Father on His throne.
REVELATION 3:21 NKJV

For you have need of endurance, so that after you have
done the will of God, you may receive the promise.
HEBREWS 10:36 NKJV

I have fought the good fight, I have finished the race,
I have kept the faith. Now there is in store for me the
crown of righteousness, which the Lord, the righteous
Judge, will award to me on that day—and not only to
me, but also to all who have longed for his appearing.
2 TIMOTHY 4:7–8 NIV

Therefore put on the full armor of God, so that when the day of evil comes, you may be able to stand your ground, and after you have done everything, to stand.
EPHESIANS 6:13 NIV

Everyone who competes in the games goes into strict training. They do it to get a crown that will not last; but we do it to get a crown that will last forever.
1 CORINTHIANS 9:25 NIV

He will give eternal life to those who keep on doing good, seeking after the glory and honor and immortality that God offers.
ROMANS 2:7 NLT

God blesses those who patiently endure testing and temptation. Afterward they will receive the crown of life that God has promised to those who love him.
JAMES 1:12 NLT

And let us run with endurance the race God has set
before us. We do this by keeping our eyes on Jesus, the
champion who initiates and perfects our faith.
HEBREWS 12:1–2 NLT

All good athletes train hard. They do it for a
gold medal that tarnishes and fades.
You're after one that's gold eternally.
1 CORINTHIANS 9:25 MSG

We have come to share in Christ if we hold
firmly till the end the confidence we had at first.
HEBREWS 3:14 NIV

We're depending on GOD;
he's everything we need.
PSALM 33:20 MSG

Physical Health

Your Amazing Body

*Do you not know that your body is a temple of the Holy Spirit,
who is in you, whom you have received from God?
You are not your own; you were bought at a price.
Therefore honor God with your body.*
1 CORINTHIANS 6:19–20 NIV

Our bodies are an amazing gift from God. But these incredible bodies aren't maintenance-free. Just as we are to be good stewards of our resources of time and money, we should also be good stewards of our bodies. God's Word calls our bodies His temple.

When we are young, our bodies function so well that many of us make the mistake of abusing them. We exercise too much (or not enough), make poor food choices, and try to operate on too little sleep. If you're living this way now, you may not realize the toll your lifestyle is taking on your body, but someday it might be too late to reverse some of the results!

God designed our earthly bodies to work for us for many, many years. That's why it's important to treat them with care and respect. Good habits like regular, moderate exercise, quality nutrition, and adequate sleep are simple things, but they pay enormous dividends. Honor God with your body and it will reward you by functioning precisely as the amazing creation God designed it to be.

*"Physical training is good, but training for
godliness is much better, promising benefits
in this life and in the life to come."*
1 TIMOTHY 4:8 NLT

*Dear friend, I hope all is well with you and that you
are as healthy in body as you are strong in spirit.*
3 JOHN 1:2 NLT

*You don't know the first thing about tomorrow.
You're nothing but a wisp of fog, catching a brief
bit of sun before disappearing. Instead, make it
a habit to say, "If the Master wills it and
we're still alive, we'll do this or that."*
JAMES 4:14–15 MSG

*Charm can mislead and beauty soon fades.
The woman to be admired and praised is
the woman who lives in the Fear-of-GOD.*
PROVERBS 31:30 MSG

"The LORD does not look at the things man looks at.
Man looks at the outward appearance,
but the LORD looks at the heart."
1 SAMUEL 16:7 NIV

Therefore, if anyone is in Christ,
he is a new creation; old things have passed away;
behold, all things have become new.
2 CORINTHIANS 5:17 NKJV

"Do not judge according to appearance,
but judge with righteous judgment."
JOHN 7:24 NKJV

I also want women to dress modestly, with decency and
propriety, not with braided hair or gold or pearls or
expensive clothes, but with good deeds, appropriate
for women who profess to worship God.
1 TIMOTHY 2:9–10 NIV

*And so, dear brothers and sisters, I plead with you to
give your bodies to God. . . . Let them be a living and
holy sacrifice—the kind he will find acceptable. . . .
Don't copy the behavior and customs of this world, but
let God transform you into a new person by changing
the way you think. Then you will learn to know God's
will for you, which is good and pleasing and perfect.*
ROMANS 12:1–2 NLT

*There is no soundness in my flesh because of Your anger,
nor any health in my bones because of my sin.*
PSALM 38:3 NKJV

*Since we have these promises, dear friends, let us purify
ourselves from everything that contaminates body and
spirit, perfecting holiness out of reverence for God.*
2 CORINTHIANS 7:1 NIV

*Have mercy on me, O LORD, for I am weak;
O LORD, heal me, for my bones are troubled.*
PSALM 6:2 NKJV

Oh yes, you shaped me first inside, then out;
you formed me in my mother's womb. I thank you,
High God—you're breathtaking!
Body and soul, I am marvelously made!
PSALM 139:13–14 MSG

No wonder my heart is glad, and my tongue
shouts his praises! My body rests in hope.
ACTS 2:26 NLT

Remember that your bodies are created
with the same dignity as the Master's body.
1 CORINTHIANS 6:15 MSG

As was the man of dust, so also are those who are
made of dust; and as is the heavenly Man,
so also are those who are heavenly.
1 CORINTHIANS 15:48 NKJV

Turning Worry into Prayer

So let us come boldly to the throne of our gracious God.
There we will receive his mercy, and we will find
grace to help us when we need it most.
HEBREWS 4:16 NLT

Michael was worried. It had been weeks since he
applied to graduate school, and he still hadn't
heard a thing. What if he didn't get accepted into his
program? Then he'd have to start paying back student
loans right away. What if he couldn't get a job because
he lacked experience? What if he would never be able
to move out of his parents' house? Before long Michael
would break out in a sweat, sure he was doomed to flip
burgers for the rest of his life.

Sound familiar? When we get carried away with
worry, it becomes like a runaway freight train, gaining
speed and momentum at every turn. No matter what
worries you, the next time you are overcome with worry,
instead of getting carried away with what-ifs, turn that
worry into a prayer. Then relax and take a deep breath.
You can be sure that your worries and your future are
safe with God.

Are any of you suffering hardships? You should pray.
Are any of you happy? You should sing praises.
JAMES 5:13 NLT

Because of Christ and our faith in him, we can now
come boldly and confidently into God's presence.
EPHESIANS 3:12 NLT

We're bold and free before God! We're able to stretch our
hands out and receive what we asked for because we're
doing what he said, doing what pleases him.
1 JOHN 3:21–22 MSG

The moment we get tired in the waiting, God's Spirit
is right alongside helping us along. If we don't know
how or what to pray, it doesn't matter. He does our
praying in and for us, making prayer out of our
wordless sighs, our aching groans.
ROMANS 8:26 MSG

Is any one of you sick? He should call the elders of the church to pray over him and anoint him with oil in the name of the Lord. And the prayer offered in faith will make the sick person well; the Lord will raise him up. If he has sinned, he will be forgiven.
JAMES 5:14–15 NIV

I desire therefore that the men pray everywhere, lifting up holy hands, without wrath and doubting.
1 TIMOTHY 2:8 NKJV

"If you, then, though you are evil, know how to give good gifts to your children, how much more will your Father in heaven give good gifts to those who ask him!"
MATTHEW 7:11 NIV

Don't quit in hard times; pray all the harder.
ROMANS 12:12 MSG

The LORD is near to all who call on him,
to all who call on him in truth.
PSALM 145:18 NIV

Therefore I say to you, whatever things you ask
when you pray, believe that you receive them,
and you will have them.
MARK 11:24 NKJV

"When you call on me, when you come and pray to me,
I'll listen. When you come looking for me,
you'll find me."
JEREMIAH 29:12–13 MSG

"You haven't done this before. Ask, using my name, and
you will receive, and you will have abundant joy."
JOHN 16:24 NLT

"Before they call I will answer;
while they are still speaking I will hear."
ISAIAH 65:24 NIV

"Ask, and it will be given to you; seek,
and you will find; knock, and it will be opened to you."
MATTHEW 7:7 NKJV

Confess your trespasses to one another, and pray for
one another, that you may be healed. The effective,
fervent prayer of a righteous man avails much.
JAMES 5:16 NKJV

"I also tell you this: If two of you agree here on earth
concerning anything you ask, my Father in heaven will
do it for you. For where two or three gather together as
my followers, I am there among them."
MATTHEW 18:19–20 NLT

Who's on the Throne?

When Jesus heard this, he said to him, "You still lack one thing. Sell everything you have and give to the poor, and you will have treasure in heaven. Then come, follow me."
LUKE 18:22 NIV

When the rich young ruler approached Jesus, he was sure he'd covered all the bases. The young man knew the law, and had followed it to the letter since he was a boy. However, Jesus threw him a curveball. "All this stuff you love," Jesus said, "get rid of it. Then follow me." Jesus' candid answer made the young man very sad because he had a lot of stuff he loved. He'd arrived. He was, perhaps, at the pinnacle of his career. Who was Jesus to ask him to give it all away?

Scripture tells us that anything we put in place of Christ on His throne in our lives is idolatry. We, as humans, are easily distracted—by wealth, material success, fame. . .the things we often envy in others when we don't possess them ourselves. The truth is, in the light of eternity, these things are worthless.

Is there anything in your life that is taking the place of Jesus? What is He asking you to give up? The cost of following Him is high, but the rewards are eternal and far too incredible for words.

*"But don't be so concerned about perishable things
like food. Spend your energy seeking the eternal life
that the Son of Man can give you. For God the
Father has given me the seal of his approval."*
JOHN 6:27 NLT

*Now we live with great expectation, and we
have a priceless inheritance—an inheritance that
is kept in heaven for you, pure and undefiled,
beyond the reach of change and decay.*
1 PETER 1:3–4 NLT

*"For God so loved the world that He gave His
only begotten Son, that whoever believes in Him
should not perish but have everlasting life."*
JOHN 3:16 NKJV

*This truth gives them confidence that they have
eternal life, which God—who does not lie—
promised them before the world began.*
TITUS 1:2 NLT

*"For where your treasure is,
there your heart will be also."*
LUKE 12:34 NKJV

*He has given us eternal life, and this life is in his Son.
Whoever has the Son has life; whoever does not have
God's Son does not have life. I have written this to you
who believe in the name of the Son of God, so that you
may know you have eternal life.*
1 JOHN 5:11–13 NLT

*"The kingdom of heaven is like treasure hidden in a
field, which a man found and hid; and for joy over it he
goes and sells all that he has and buys that field."*
MATTHEW 13:44 NKJV

*In this way they will lay up treasure for themselves as
a firm foundation for the coming age, so that they may
take hold of the life that is truly life.*
1 TIMOTHY 6:19 NIV

Work hard for sin your whole life and your pension is death. But God's gift is real life, eternal life, delivered by Jesus, our Master.
ROMANS 6:23 MSG

"The righteous will go into eternal life."
MATTHEW 25:46 NLT

"The water I give will be an artesian spring within, gushing fountains of endless life."
JOHN 4:14 MSG

Make no mistake: In the end you get what's coming to you—Real Life for those who work on God's side.
ROMANS 2:7 MSG

*And when the Chief Shepherd appears, you will
receive the crown of glory that will never fade away.*
1 PETER 5:4 NIV

*So that, having been justified by his grace, we might
become heirs having the hope of eternal life.*
TITUS 3:7 NIV

*"Now this is eternal life: that they may know you, the
only true God, and Jesus Christ, whom you have sent."*
JOHN 17:3 NIV

*For we know that if our earthly house, this tent, is
destroyed, we have a building from God, a house not
made with hands, eternal in the heavens.*
2 CORINTHIANS 5:1 NKJV

Sometimes You Need a Hand

Aaron and Hur held his hands up—one on one side,
one on the other—so that his hands remained steady till sunset.
EXODUS 17:12 NIV

It was a simple job. As long as he stood on a hill and held up his hands, the Israelites would have the upper hand in their battle with the Amalekites. If Moses lowered his hands, the Amalekites would take the lead. Despite the simplicity of his task, Moses soon learned he needed help. That's where his brother Aaron and his friend Hur came in. They put a rock under Moses so he could rest, and then stood beside him, holding up his hands for the rest of the battle so that the Israelites would prevail. God could have let the Israelites win without Moses' hands in the air. But perhaps God chose to accomplish it this way so that we would appreciate the value of a helping hand.

There are just some things in this life that are too hard to do alone. Like Moses, we all need a helping hand from time to time. And when we allow others to help us, we are not the only ones who receive a blessing. Often, when we allow someone to do something for us, they are blessed as much or more than we are. When you need help, don't be afraid to ask. Sometimes it can mean the difference between victory and defeat.

If it is possible, as much as depends on you,
live peaceably with all men.
ROMANS 12:18 NKJV

For everything we know about God's Word is summed
up in a single sentence: Love others as you love yourself.
GALATIANS 5:14 MSG

Finally, all of you be of one mind,
having compassion for one another; love as brothers,
be tenderhearted, be courteous.
1 PETER 3:8 NKJV

You do well when you complete the Royal Rule of the
Scriptures: "Love others as you love yourself."
JAMES 2:8 MSG

Anyone who hates a brother or sister is a murderer,
and you know very well that eternal life
and murder don't go together.
1 JOHN 3:15 MSG

Work at living in peace with everyone,
and work at living a holy life, for those
who are not holy will not see the Lord.
HEBREWS 12:14 NLT

Therefore let us pursue the things which make for peace
and the things by which one may edify another.
ROMANS 14:19 NKJV

Love is patient, love is kind. It does not envy,
it does not boast, it is not proud. It is not rude,
it is not self-seeking, it is not easily angered,
it keeps no record of wrongs.
1 CORINTHIANS 13:4–5 NIV

You shall not take vengeance, nor bear any
grudge against the children of your people,
but you shall love your neighbor as yourself.
LEVITICUS 19:18 NKJV

My beloved friends, let us continue to love each other
since love comes from God. Everyone who loves is born
of God and experiences a relationship with God.
1 JOHN 4:7 MSG

Share each other's burdens,
and in this way obey the law of Christ.
GALATIANS 6:2 NLT

"You have heard the law that says, 'Love your neighbor'
and hate your enemy. But I say, love your enemies!
Pray for those who persecute you!"
MATTHEW 5:43–44 NLT

Rejoice with those who rejoice;
mourn with those who mourn.
ROMANS 12:15 NIV

This is the message you heard from the beginning:
We should love one another.
1 JOHN 3:11 NIV

Respect everyone, and love your Christian brothers
and sisters. Fear God, and respect the king.
1 PETER 2:17 NLT

"So if you are presenting a sacrifice at the altar in
the Temple and you suddenly remember that someone
has something against you, leave your sacrifice there
at the altar. Go and be reconciled to that person.
Then come and offer your sacrifice to God."
MATTHEW 5:23–24 NLT

Focus Time

*In the morning, O LORD, you hear my voice; in the morning
I lay my requests before you and wait in expectation.*
PSALM 5:3 NIV

No team takes the field without first meeting in the locker room for a pregame talk. No actor takes the stage without first getting into character. It would be foolish to build a house without consulting with an architect and drawing up plans. Adequate preparation is the first essential step for any successful endeavor.

Throughout his earthly ministry, Jesus modeled this principle. He was an incredibly busy man. There were disciples to train, people to heal, and children to bless. No matter what He did or where He traveled, something or someone seemed to always need attention. But despite the many demands placed on Him, scripture tells us that Jesus got up early in the morning to take time to meet His Father in prayer.

What is the first thing you do each morning? Many of us hit the ground running, armed with to-do lists a mile long. Unfortunately, this means that we often lack focus and fall into bed at night wondering if we really accomplished anything at all. While it doesn't ensure perfection, setting aside even a short time each morning to focus on the Father can help prepare us to live for Him.

How will you start your day today?

Then Jehoshaphat added,
"But first let's find out what the LORD says."
1 KINGS 22:5 NLT

You will guide me with Your counsel.
PSALM 73:24 NKJV

Very early in the morning, while it was still dark,
Jesus got up, left the house and went off to
a solitary place, where he prayed.
MARK 1:35 NIV

I will instruct you and teach
you in the way you should go.
PSALM 32:8 NKJV

I rise before the dawning of the morning,
and cry for help; I hope in Your word.
PSALM 119:147 NKJV

Strong God, I'm watching you do it, I can always
count on you—God, my dependable love.
PSALM 59:17 MSG

Through the night my soul longs for you.
Deep from within me my spirit reaches out to you.
ISAIAH 26:9 MSG

Satisfy us in the morning with your unfailing love, that
we may sing for joy and be glad all our days.
PSALM 90:14 NIV

O LORD, be gracious to us; we have waited for You.
Be their arm every morning, our salvation
also in the time of trouble.
ISAIAH 33:2 NKJV

Let the morning bring me word of your unfailing love,
for I have put my trust in you. Show me the way I
should go, for to you I lift up my soul.
PSALM 143:8 NIV

God's loyal love couldn't have run out, his merciful
love couldn't have dried up. They're created new every
morning. How great your faithfulness!
LAMENTATIONS 3:22–23 MSG

Lead me by your truth and teach me, for you are the
God who saves me. All day long I put my hope in you.
PSALM 25:5 NLT

"Come to me. Get away with me and you'll recover your life. I'll show you how to take a real rest."
MATTHEW 11:29 MSG

Let the word of Christ dwell in you richly as you teach and admonish one another with all wisdom, and as you sing psalms, hymns and spiritual songs with gratitude in your hearts to God.
COLOSSIANS 3:16 NIV

Teach us to realize the brevity of life, so that we may grow in wisdom
PSALM 90:12 NLT

Focus on reading the Scriptures to the church, encouraging the believers, and teaching them.
1 TIMOTHY 4:13 NLT

Who Do You Believe?

*"You will know the truth,
and the truth will set you free."*
JOHN 8:32 NLT

Todd loved baseball and really hoped to play in high school, but his eighth grade gym teacher talked him out of it. "Give it up now, Todd—you definitely don't have what it takes to make the team." Todd got the message loud and clear. He went through all four years of high school never bothering to try out. Imagine his surprise when he became the star player on his intramural softball team in college.

Have you ever believed a lie about yourself? Moses did. In Exodus, when God called him to lead the children of Israel, Moses responded that he was "slow of speech." He doubted that people would listen to him (see Exodus 3–4). However, a different portrait of Moses is painted in the book of Acts. In Stephen's speech to the Sanhedrin, he says that Moses was "powerful in speech and action" (see Acts 7:20–36).

Many of us struggle to believe the truth about ourselves, just like Moses did. The lies we believe can come from many places, but ultimately, they come from Satan himself. What lies do you believe about yourself? How might those lies be preventing you from experiencing God's plan for *your* life?

Lead me in Your truth and teach me,
for You are the God of my salvation;
on You I wait all the day.
PSALM 25:5 NKJV

Jesus answered, "I am the way and the truth and the
life. No one comes to the Father except through me."
JOHN 14:6 NIV

Truth shall spring out of the earth,
and righteousness shall look down from heaven.
PSALM 85:11 NKJV

He will wear righteousness like a belt
and truth like an undergarment.
ISAIAH 11:5 NLT

Truth lasts; lies are here today,
gone tomorrow.
PROVERBS 12:19 MSG

We are from God, and whoever knows God listens to us;
but whoever is not from God does not listen to us.
This is how we recognize the Spirit of truth
and the spirit of falsehood.
1 JOHN 4:6 NIV

An intelligent person is always eager to take in more
truth; fools feed on fast-food fads and fancies.
PROVERBS 15:14 MSG

But for those who are self-seeking and who reject the
truth and follow evil, there will be wrath and anger.
ROMANS 2:8 NIV

I have chosen the way of truth;
your judgments I have laid before me.
PSALM 119:30 NKJV

"And you shall know the truth,
and the truth shall make you free."
JOHN 8:32 NKJV

They exchanged the truth of God for a lie, and
worshiped and served created things rather than the
Creator—who is forever praised. Amen.
ROMANS 1:25 NIV

"When the Spirit of truth comes, he will guide you into
all truth. He will not speak on his own but will tell you
what he has heard. He will tell you about the future."
JOHN 16:13 NLT

"Make them holy—consecrated—with the truth;
your word is consecrating truth."
JOHN 17:17 MSG

[Love] does not rejoice about injustice
but rejoices whenever the truth wins out.
1 CORINTHIANS 13:6 NLT

Stand your ground, putting on the belt of truth
and the body armor of God's righteousness.
EPHESIANS 6:14 NLT

I haven't been writing this to tell you something you
don't know, but to confirm the truth you do know,
and to remind you that the truth doesn't breed lies.
1 JOHN 2:21 MSG

Wisdom

Wisdom for Life

My son, if you accept my words and store up my commands within you. . .then you will understand the fear of the LORD and find the knowledge of God.
PROVERBS 2:1, 5 NIV

Even though we have many different types of electronic communication at our fingertips, it's still fun to receive a letter in the mail. Letters are especially sweet when they come from someone who loves us.

King Solomon wrote a wonderful letter to his sons in the Bible—better known as the book of Proverbs. At its core, this little gem is a heartfelt love letter from a father to his children—not only from Solomon to his sons, but from God to us.

Proverbs contains an abundance of short sayings that are as relevant to us now as they surely were to Solomon's sons centuries ago. The wisdom of Proverbs can apply to every area of our lives. It addresses everything from relationships to our finances and to our work habits.

A righteous man is cautious in friendship (Proverbs 12:26 NIV). *A greedy man brings trouble to his family* (Proverbs 15:27 NIV). *Commit to the LORD whatever you do, and your plans will succeed* (Proverbs 16:3 NIV).

These nuggets in scripture are timeless truths, guidelines for living, ways to increase your chances of success in life. Biblical success—righteousness, integrity, honesty, wisdom—that's yours for a lifetime.

A wise youth harvests in the summer,
but one who sleeps during harvest is a disgrace.
PROVERBS 10:5 NLT

Who is wise? Let him understand these things.
Who is prudent? Let him know them. For the ways
of the LORD are right; the righteous walk in them,
but transgressors stumble in them.
HOSEA 14:9 NKJV

The way of a fool is right in his own eyes,
but he who heeds counsel is wise.
PROVERBS 12:15 NKJV

Prudent people don't flaunt their knowledge;
talkative fools broadcast their silliness.
PROVERBS 12:23 MSG

Lazy people want much but get little,
but those who work hard will prosper.
PROVERBS 13:4 NLT

Plans fail for lack of counsel,
but with many advisers they succeed.
PROVERBS 15:22 NIV

I will instruct you and teach you in the way you
should go; I will counsel you and watch over you.
PSALM 32:8 NIV

The teaching of the wise is a fountain of life,
turning a man from the snares of death.
PROVERBS 13:14 NIV

Even fools are thought wise when they keep silent;
with their mouths shut, they seem intelligent.
PROVERBS 17:28 NLT

"Men and women who have lived wisely and well
will shine brilliantly, like the cloudless, star-strewn
night skies. And those who put others on the right
path to life will glow like stars forever."
DANIEL 12:3 MSG

Of what use is money in the hand of a fool,
since he has no desire to get wisdom?
PROVERBS 17:16 NIV

We humans keep brainstorming options and plans,
but GOD's purpose prevails.
PROVERBS 19:21 MSG

He who follows righteousness and mercy finds life,
righteousness, and honor.
PROVERBS 21:21 NKJV

Choose a good reputation over great riches;
being held in high esteem is better than silver or gold.
PROVERBS 22:1 NLT

Wisdom and knowledge will be the stability
of your times, and the strength of salvation;
the fear of the LORD is His treasure.
ISAIAH 33:6 NKJV

Just as water mirrors your face,
so your face mirrors your heart.
PROVERBS 27:19 MSG

Little Things Become
Big Things

"His master replied, 'Well done, good and faithful servant!
You have been faithful with a few things; I will put you in
charge of many things. Come and share your master's happiness!'"
MATTHEW 25:23 NIV

When Megan saw a newspaper ad looking for a floral designer at an upscale flower shop, she was confident that it was the perfect job for her. She loved to design trendy and unique arrangements and had even sold some to a couple of her mom's friends. Unfortunately, the shop manager wouldn't hire her because she lacked formal training.

Megan faced a reality that is common to many new grads. "We'd love to hire you, but you lack experience." But just how is a person supposed to get experience if no one ever hires her?

Jesus addresses this issue from a spiritual perspective when He tells the parable of the talents in Matthew 25. There He says that as we demonstrate trustworthiness with little things, God will gradually increase our responsibilities, entrusting us with bigger and more important tasks.

If you lack experience, there are many things you can do to show your trustworthiness. Take on small jobs in your field of interest. Look for places to volunteer your services. Pray for opportunities to showcase your talents. Those little efforts will be rewarded, and after a while they'll add up to a lifetime of worthwhile experience.

Whatever your hand finds to do,
do it with your might.
ECCLESIASTES 9:10 NKJV

Even when we were with you, we gave you this rule:
"If a man will not work, he shall not eat."
2 THESSALONIANS 3:10 NIV

Hard work always pays off;
mere talk puts no bread on the table.
PROVERBS 14:23 MSG

It is [the LORD your God] who blesses you with
bountiful harvests and gives you success in all your
work. This festival will be a time of great joy for all.
DEUTERONOMY 16:15 NLT

*"But you, be strong and do not let your hands be weak,
for your work shall be rewarded!"*
2 Chronicles 15:7 nkjv

*You worked hard and deserve all you've got coming.
Enjoy the blessing! Revel in the goodness!*
Psalm 128:2 msg

*So, my dear brothers and sisters, be strong
and immovable. Always work enthusiastically
for the Lord, for you know that nothing you
do for the Lord is ever useless.*
1 Corinthians 15:58 nlt

*Don't be too fond of sleep; you'll end up in the poorhouse.
Wake up and get up; then there'll be food on the table.*
Proverbs 20:13 msg

*You have six days each week for your ordinary work,
but the seventh day is a Sabbath day of
rest dedicated to the LORD your God.*
EXODUS 20:9–10 NLT

*He who works his land will have abundant food,
but he who chases fantasies lacks judgment.*
PROVERBS 12:11 NIV

*If you are a thief, quit stealing. Instead, use
your hands for good hard work, and then
give generously to others in need.*
EPHESIANS 4:28 NLT

*Now he who plants and he who waters are one,
and each one will receive his own reward
according to his own labor.*
1 CORINTHIANS 3:8 NKJV

*Make it your ambition to lead a quiet life,
to mind your own business and to work with
your hands, just as we told you, so that your daily
life may win the respect of outsiders and so that
you will not be dependent on anybody.*
1 THESSALONIANS 4:11–12 NIV

*And let the beauty of the LORD our God be upon us,
and establish the work of our hands for us;
yes, establish the work of our hands.*
PSALM 90:17 NKJV

*Lazy people are soon poor;
hard workers get rich.*
PROVERBS 10:4 NLT

*GOD, your God, has blessed you
in everything you have done.*
DEUTERONOMY 2:7 MSG

Choose Praise

Because your love is better than life, my lips will glorify you.
I will praise you as long as I live,
and in your name I will lift up my hands.
PSALM 63:3–4 NIV

Kendra's father was one of her best friends. They often worked side by side—putting up Christmas lights, planting flowers in the garden, or puttering in the basement. When her father suffered a stroke at age fifty-seven, Kendra was shocked. Her heart broke to see him confined to a hospital bed, struggling to remember familiar names and complete simple tasks. Kendra began slipping into feelings of depression, until something her mother said changed everything.

"Even though I don't understand why this happened," her mother said through tears, "instead of asking why, I *choose* to praise."

It's natural to praise God when life is going our way. We are thankful, joyful, obedient—God has blessed us! But when faced with difficult circumstances, when our questions remain unanswered, it is easy to become hopeless and depressed.

No matter what life brings, it is important to remember that we always have a choice. We can choose to resign ourselves to defeat, becoming bitter and miserable; or we can praise the One who knows best, who loves us the very most. Praising God doesn't change our circumstances, but it does change our hearts. And that changes everything.

I will praise you forever for what you have done;
in your name I will hope, for your name is good.
I will praise you in the presence of your saints.
PSALM 52:9 NIV

"The LORD is my strength and song, and He has
become my salvation; He is my God, and I will praise
Him; my father's God, and I will exalt Him."
EXODUS 15:2 NKJV

All the nations you made will come and bow before you,
Lord; they will praise your holy name.
PSALM 86:9 NLT

Give to the LORD the glory he deserves!
Bring your offering and come into his presence.
Worship the LORD in all his holy splendor.
1 CHRONICLES 16:29 NLT

*Therefore by Him let us continually offer
the sacrifice of praise to God, that is, the fruit of our lips,
giving thanks to His name.*
HEBREWS 13:15 NKJV

*I will proclaim the name of the LORD.
Oh, praise the greatness of our God!*
DEUTERONOMY 32:3 NIV

*Break forth into joy, sing together. . .
for the LORD has comforted His people.*
ISAIAH 52:9 NKJV

*Worship the LORD with gladness.
Come before him, singing with joy.*
PSALM 100:2 NLT

"The LORD lives! Praise be to my Rock!
Exalted be God, the Rock, my Savior!"
2 SAMUEL 22:47 NIV

"My soul magnifies the Lord."
LUKE 1:46 NKJV

For great is his love toward us, and the faithfulness
of the LORD endures forever. Praise the LORD.
PSALM 117:2 NIV

To all who mourn in Israel, he will give a crown
of beauty for ashes, a joyous blessing instead of
mourning, festive praise instead of despair. In their
righteousness, they will be like great oaks that the
LORD has planted for his own glory.
ISAIAH 61:3 NLT

How blessed is God! And what a blessing he is!
He's the Father of our Master, Jesus Christ,
and takes us to the high places of blessing in him.
EPHESIANS 1:3 MSG

Why are you down in the dumps, dear soul?
Why are you crying the blues? Fix my eyes on God—
soon I'll be praising again. He puts a smile on my face.
He's my God.
PSALM 42:11 MSG

I'll bless you every day,
and keep it up from now to eternity.
PSALM 145:2 MSG

And here we are, O God, our God,
giving thanks to you, praising your splendid Name.
1 CHRONICLES 29:13 MSG